To parents and teachers

We hope you and the children will enjoy reading this story in either English or French. The story is simple, but not *simplified,* so the language of the French and the English is quite natural, although there is lots of repetition.

At the back of the book is a small picture dictionary with the key words and how to pronounce them. There is also a simple pronunciation guide to the whole story on the last page.

Here are a few suggestions on using the book:

- Read the story aloud in English first, to get to know it. Treat it like any other picture book: look at the pictures, talk about the story and the characters, and so on.

- Then look at the picture dictionary and say the French names for the key words. Ask the children to repeat them. Concentrate on speaking the words out loud, rather than reading them.

- Go back and read the story again, this time in English *and* French. Don't worry if your pronunciation isn't quite correct. Just have fun trying it out. Check the guide at the back of the book, if necessary, but you'll soon pick up how to say the French words.

- When you think you and the children are ready, you can try reading the story in French only. Ask the children to say it with you. Ask them to read it only if they are eager to try. The spelling could be confusing and put them off.

- Above all, encourage the children to try it, and give lots of praise. Little children are usually quite unself-conscious and this is excellent for building up confidence in a foreign language.

First edition for the United States, its dependencies, Canada, and the Philippines published in 2006 by Barron's Educational Series, Inc. Text and illustrations © Copyright 2005 by *b small publishing*

Address all inquiries to:
Barron's Educational Series, Inc. • 250 Wireless Boulevard • Hauppauge, New York 11788 • **http://www.barronseduc.com**

ISBN-13: 978-0-7641-5874-2   ISBN-10: 0-7641-5874-0
Library of Congress Catalog Card Number 2005921560

Printed in China
9 8 7 6 5 4 3 2 1

George, the goldfish

Georges, le poisson rouge

Lone Morton

Pictures by Leighton Noyes
French by Marie-Thérèse Bougard

Harry has a goldfish.
His name is George.

Harry a un poisson rouge.
Il s'appelle Georges.

George swims around and around in his bowl. Harry loves to watch him.

Georges fait le tour de son aquarium. Harry adore le regarder.

But one day Harry's goldfish dies.

Mais un jour, le poisson rouge
de Harry meurt.

Harry is very sad and he cries.

Harry est très triste et il pleure.

His mother hugs him.
"George made you happy."

Sa maman lui fait un gros câlin.
"Tu aimais bien Georges, hein"?

"We will bury him in the garden," she says. "And he will make the garden happy."

"On va l'enterrer dans le jardin", dit-elle. "Et il rendra le jardin heureux".

Harry paints a small box.

Harry peint une petite boîte.

He puts George on some leaves
in the box.

Il pose Georges sur des feuilles
dans la boîte.

It's summer.
Harry and his mother dig
a hole under the tree.

C'est l'été.
Harry et sa maman creusent
un trou sous l'arbre.

Harry puts the box in the hole
and covers it with earth.

Harry met la boîte dans le trou
et la recouvre de terre.

His mother plants three flower bulbs.

Sa maman plante trois oignons de fleurs.

"Now George will help the garden to grow. Wait and see," says Harry's mother.

"Maintenant Georges va aider le jardin à pousser. Tu vas voir", dit la maman de Harry.

In the autumn, all the leaves fall from the tree.

Pendant l'automne, toutes les feuilles tombent de l'arbre.

In the winter, it is cold and it snows.

Pendant l'hiver, il fait froid et il neige.

And then, in the spring, three little shoots appear.

Et puis, au printemps, trois petites pousses sortent du terre.

Every day, they grow…
Tous les jours, elles poussent…

and grow…
et poussent…

and grow.
et poussent.

One morning, Harry looks out the
window and sees three yellow flowers.

Un matin, Harry regarde par la
fenêtre et voit trois fleurs jaunes.

Harry and his mother run out into the garden.

Harry et sa maman se précipitent dans le jardin.

"You see, George helped them to grow tall and beautiful," says his mother.

"Tu vois, Georges les a aidées à devenir grandes et belles", dit sa maman.

Harry smiles.

Harry sourit.

Pronouncing French

Don't worry if your pronunciation isn't quite correct.
The important thing is to be willing to try. The pronunciation
guide here will help but it cannot be completely accurate:

• Read the guide as naturally as possible, as if it were English.

• Put stress on the letters in *italics*, as in poo-*seh*.

If you can, ask a French person to help, and move on as soon as
possible to speaking the words without the guide.

Note: French adjectives usually have two forms, one for masculine
and one for feminine nouns, as in **grand** and **grande.**

Words Les mots

leh moh

goldfish
le poisson rouge

leh pwah-*soh* roojsh

mother
la maman

lah mam-*ah*

tree
l'arbre
larbr'

tall
grand/grande
grah/grand

leaf/leaves
la feuille/les feuilles
lah feh-*yee*/leh feh-*yee*

flower
la fleur
lah flurr

garden
le jardin
leh shar-*dah*

beautiful
beau/belle
boh/bel

to grow
pousser
poo-*seh*

happy
heureux/
heureuse
er-*reh*/er-*rehz*

to smile
sourire
soo-*reer*

sad
triste
treest

to cry
pleurer
pler-*reh*

spring
le printemps

leh pran-*tah*

summer
l'été

leh-*teh*

autumn
l'automne

low-*ton*

winter
l'hiver

lee-*vair*

cold
froid/froide

frwah/frwad

it snows
il neige

eel neshj

A simple guide to pronouncing this French story

Georges le poisson rouge
zhorjsh leh pwah-*soh* roojsh

Harry a un poisson rouge.
a*ree* ah ahn pwah-*soh* roojsh

Il s'appelle Georges.
eel sa*pel* zhorjsh

Georges fait le tour de son aquarium.
zhorjsh feh leh toor deh son akwah-ree-*oom*

Harry adore le regarder.
a*ree* a*door* leh reh-gard-*eh*

Mais un jour, le poisson rouge de Harry meurt.
meh ahn zhoor leh pwah-*soh* roojsh deh a*ree* murr

Harry est très triste et il pleure.
a*ree* eh trch treest eh eel plurr

Sa maman lui fait un gros câlin.
sah mam-*ah* lwee feh ahn groh ka*lah*

"Tu aimais bien Georges, hein"?
too eh-*meh* bee-*ah* zhorjsh, ahn

"On va l'enterrer dans le jardin", dit-elle.
oh vah lon-tair-*eh* dah leh zhar-*dah*, deet-el

"Et il rendra le jardin heureux".
eh eel ron*drah* leh zhar-*dah* er-*reh*

Harry peint une petite boîte.
a*ree* pah oon p'*teet* bwat

Il pose Georges sur des feuilles dans la boîte.
eel pohz zhorjsh soor deh feh-*yee* dah lah bwat

C'est l'été.
seh leh-*teh*

Harry et sa maman creusent un trou sous l'arbre.
a*ree* eh sah mam-*ah* krerz ahn troo soo larbr'

Harry met la boîte dans le trou et la recouvre de terre.
a*ree* meh lah bwat dah leh troo eh lah re*koovr*' der tair

Sa maman plante trois oignons de fleurs.
sah mam-*ah* plohnt trwahz on-*yoh* deh flurr

"Maintenant Georges va aider le jardin à pousser.
man-t'n-*ah* zhoorjsh vah eh-*deh* leh zhar*dah* ah poo-*seh*

Tu vas voir", dit la maman de Harry.
too vah vwah, dee lah mam-*ah* deh a*ree*

Pendant l'automne, toutes les feuilles tombent de l'arbre.
pon-*doh* low-*ton*, toot leh feh-*yee* tomb deh larbr'

Pendant l'hiver, il fait froid et il neige.
pon-*doh* lee-*vair*, eel feh frwah eh eel neshj

Et puis, au printemps, trois petites pousses sortent du terre.
eh pwee, oh prah-*toh*, trwah p'*teet* poos sort doo tair

Tous les jours, elles poussent, et poussent, et poussent.
too leh zhoor, el poos, eh poos, eh poos

Un matin, Harry regarde par la fenêtre
ahn ma*tah*, a*ree* reh-*gard* pah lah f'*netr*'

et voit trois fleurs jaunes.
eh vwah trwah flurr zhown

Harry et sa maman se précipitent dans le jardin.
a*ree* eh sah mam-*ah* seh preh-see-*peet* dah leh zhar-*dah*

"Tu vois, Georges les a aidées
too vwah, zhoorjsh leh-zah eh-*deh*

à devenir grandes et belles", dit sa maman.
ah dev'*neer* grand eh bel, dee sah mam-*ah*

Harry sourit.
a*ree* soo*ree*